Dogs Rule!

The Rules,
Wisdom, and Witticisms
That Go Along with Being a Dog

illustrations by
Setsu Broderick

as told to Bob Lovka

Ruth Berman, editor-in-chief
Nick Clemente, special consultant
Book design and layout by Michele Lanci-Altomare and Victor W. Perry

Library of Congress Cataloging-in-Publication Data

Lovka, Bob, Date.
    Dogs rule! : the rules, wisdom, and witticisms that go along with being a dog / as told to Bob Lovka ; illustrations by Setsu Broderick.
        p.   cm.
    ISBN 1-889540-32-3 (softcover : alk. paper)
    1. Dogs--Humor.   I. Title.
    PN6231.D68 L68   2000
    818'.5407--dc21   00-39297
                                                                                                                  CIP

BowTie™ Press
3 Burroughs
Irvine, California 92618

Manufactured in the United States of America
10 9 8 7 6 5 4 3 2 1

To Marge at Angel Puss and Pooch Rescue,
the best mom a lost, lonely, or abandoned cat
or dog could ever find—B. L.

For Kyle, Raulie, Genna, Parker, and Wyatt —S. B.

Contents

Introduction 6

Foon's Facts and Fictions 9

Bear's Briefings 41

Dingo's Dizzy Declarations 65

Rocky's Down-Home Wisdom 91

Trigger's Talk 'n' Tales 113

Introduction

My dog, Foon, is a half-crazed, strong-willed, and occasionally jealous Lhasa apso. It's the jealousy that prompts this book.

Recently, Sonny (my cat) took pity on my ignorance about the feline world and my misreading of what cats do and why they do it. Sonny, along with a few of his friends, proceeded to explain the mysterious world of cats to me and opened my eyes to what felines are really up to and what they're thinking. The result was a scientific tome entitled *Cats Rule!*

Foon was not pleased, especially after Sonny acquired a pen name (Sunny) and started getting offers to lecture and write. "Too much attention to cats." "Who do they think they are?" "Scratch my back" were all I kept hearing. He felt it was time that dogs had their day.

Foon pointed out that dogs have a proud history of achievement and ethics; they have been man's best friend and woman's, too, since the caveperson era; and that they can be taught new tricks, performing them better than any cat could! I could see where this was going, but wanted an outside opinion.

My friend Chris Hoffman runs a great roadhouse next to the creek in Kagel Canyon. The Hideaway is also home to his big Labrador retriever, Rocky, a true canyon dog who watches over things, inspires the day's barbecue menu, and throws elaborate birthday parties for dogs and humans alike. Rocky confirmed what Foon had been saying: Dogs have natural laws and codes of honor to follow! (And their lives are ruled by savvy good sense, loyalty, and an unending quest for "people food.") Rocky gave me some down-home dog wisdom, and before I knew it, Foon, Rocky, and a whole horde of their buddies were yapping at my heels for the chance to finally tell the tales—then scratch theirs. I even met their spiritual advisor (of sorts), Kokopelli, who has graciously added his wisdom and insight into this tome.

The result is a work that will take an honored place among the great social histories and cultural accounts of the last twenty or so centuries. Foon, who hasn't worked in the literary or entertainment industries since he was Benji's agent years ago, is making me say that he was "...tireless in rounding up a plethora of diverse friends and cohorts who were eager to have this book written and the record set straight."

I took down their laws, rules, reasons, and observations of what makes a dog act as he does, listening to their explanations and recording their point of view. I felt proud to do it.

Besides, none of them would type.

Bob Lovka
Kagel Canyon
California, USA

THE CANINE GROSS-OUT GUIDE:
TIP NUMBER ONE
The more disgusting it looks,
the more fun it is to eat in front of humans.

**FOON'S
JUSTIFICATION FOR
FINGER-NIPPING**
It's love at first bite.

**FIRST LAW
OF THE COAT**
Where there's fur,
there's shedding.

THE MACMILLAN FAMILY'S DISCOVERY

The worst morning breath of the day is the one provided by the dog, but it lasts all day long.

A bad scent is in the nose of the beholder.

~F

THE UNIVERSAL POOCH PERSPECTIVE

The least intelligent dog is far brighter than the most intelligent cat.

FOON'S SLOGAN

Flea is a four-letter word.

FOON'S THEORY OF COMMUNICATION
One good sniff is worth a thousand words.

FIRST PRINCIPLE OF MEASUREMENT
Nothing smells as good an inch away as it does from a quarter inch away.

GILMAN'S ADVICE FOR SLOPPY BACHELORS
You can always blame a messy house on the dog.

THE CANINE/HUMAN CONNECTION
The one time during the evening when you finally sit back, kick off your shoes, and relax is the same time that the dog wants to go out for a walk.

FOON'S COROLLARY
A high-pitched whimper translates as "Let's go!"

THE DOUGLAS FAMILY'S DENIAL

No matter how many toys and treats you give to a dog, he never gets spoiled.

SEVEN DOG ATTRIBUTES THAT MAKE DOGS MORE THAN "JUST DOGS"

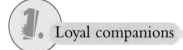 **1.** Loyal companions

 2. Outstanding hole diggers

 3. Great yodelers

4. Efficient food disposals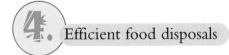

5. Fearless home alarms

6. Excellent paper shredders

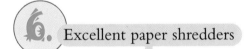

7. Tireless dishwashers

KOKOPELLI'S PHILOSOPHICAL MAXIM
The dog knows truth;
the cat, approximation.

FOON'S THEORY OF UNFAIRNESS
What the cats get away
with, the dogs don't.

FOON'S EXISTENTIAL DILEMMA
To shed or to drool—that is the question.

THE BARKLEY BUNCH'S CANINE ENTERTAINMENT EQUATION
A dog toy that promises "hours of fun" means that you're looking at 15 minutes, tops.

REGISTERED DOCUMENT 1103RD CANINE CONGRESS GUIDE TO THE BREED: MAIL CARRIER

In the diverse world of humans, there exists an especially odd breed that directly affects canine life.

These pedigreed humans—genus *Carrius mailus*—come in various sizes and shapes but all share one unusual trait: they carry their papers with them wherever they go.

Nearly every day, these obtrusive creatures show up like clockwork, spreading their pedigree notices to everyone within walking distance. This strange behavior has been studied by the greatest minds in canine psychology for over a century (in human years) and the consensus of opinion is that these people are after your job!

Vigorous barking, leaping, and snarling should be employed upon sighting this breed. Aggressiveness will drive them away temporarily, but be warned: they will be back.

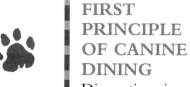

FIRST PRINCIPLE OF CANINE DINING
Dinnertime is all the time.

FOON'S FOOD MAXIM
You get the most of what you want the least.

FIRST PUPPY PRINCIPLE
Cuteness conquers all.

THE CANINE CONGRESS'S FIRST PRESCRIPTION FOR LIVING

When it comes to humans, never kiss them once; kiss them twice.

Kokopelli's Canticle to the Modern Dog
An Attempt to Set the Record Straight

Despite feline lies,
The dog is all-wise.
A hunter, companion, true friend!
A heart filled with glee,
Of high nobility,
A dog is Love without end!

But there's been talk of late
And some surveys we berate
That suggest the dog slipping in popularity!

Oh, come now...
Do you think a cat
Would guard your home?
Cheer you up
When you feel alone?
Why, the idea is utmost hilarity!

When the tally is done,
The real Number One,
The Favorite, the Best, the Sublime
Is none other than that,
Which is opposite of Cat,
The distinguished and honored Canine!

FOON'S ATTITUDE TOWARD HUMANS
Just because they're bigger doesn't mean they're better.

FIRST LAW OF TERRITORY
A dog's natural territory is the top of the bed.

Prime territory is defined as the pillow.

~F

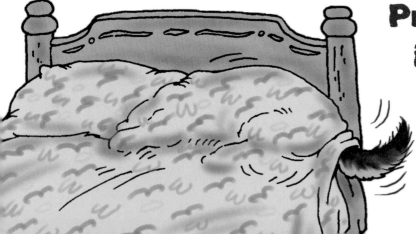

SIX FUNDAMENTAL CIVIL RIGHTS FOR TODAY'S DOG

1. The right to food, snacks, treats, and more food

2. The unlimited right to sniff

3. The right to chew anything that is not currently being used by another species

4. The right to dig in the backyard, flower garden, or potted plant of choice

5. The right to freedom of movement and resistance of travel crates

6. The right to "first call" on open car windows

FOON'S OFFICIAL POSITION ON ALL MATTERS RELATING TO DOGS
Prone

FIRST RULE OF THE FLOOR
A hard, rough-edged chew toy will find the nearest bare foot.

FOON'S REBUTTAL TO COMPLAINTS ABOUT BARKING DOGS
If a mouth is busy barking, at least it won't be biting.

ARTICLE 5 FROM THE CANINE LINGUISTIC INFORMATION FORUM
The two salt licks that are attached to your human are commonly known as "legs."

THE HOME-TRAINING POSTULATE

The only dog who will not respond to simple basic training is yours.

FIRST CANINE TRICK OF MEDICATION

Any pill hidden in a treat or piece of meat for the
purpose of administering medication can be spit
out untouched, while the treat is totally devoured.

ALFRED LORD TENNYSON'S DOG'S REFLECTION
'Tis better to have barked at nothing than never to have barked at all.

THE LOVELAND FAMILY'S DICTUM
A dog's visit to the vet takes precedence over an owner's visit to the doctor.

GENERAL DIRECTIVE FOR SLEEPING
Turn around three times and plop down.

FOON'S PSYCHIC SIGNAL
If it's time for medication, the dog disappears.

**FOON'S
RULE OF WILL**
Where there's a will,
there's a will not!

**GUIDING
PRINCIPLE FOR
DOGS AT THE
DINNER TABLE**
No dropped morsel should
ever reach the ground.

**THIRD LAW OF
CANINE CUISINE**
Any vegetables added to the dog's
food in order to enhance nutrition or
taste must be licked, tasted, rejected,
and then deposited somewhere
on the kitchen floor.

FOON'S CONCLUSION ABOUT NAMING THE DOG
The last syllable of all dog names is -*no*.

KOKOPELLI'S CANINE SEMINAR SERIES, TOPIC ONE
Should the first dog to walk on the moon howl at it?

THE CANINE BOOK OF GENESIS

Day 1: God creates dog.

Day 2: God creates man and woman.

Day 3: The bed is created and dog quickly learns to share it with man and woman.

Day 4: The ball, the stick, and the flying disc are created, giving man and woman some things to throw and dog some things to watch.

Day 5: God creates veterinary fees.

Day 6: God creates work so that man and woman can acquire a lot of money to pay veterinary fees.

Day 7: God rests but has man and woman go walk the dog.

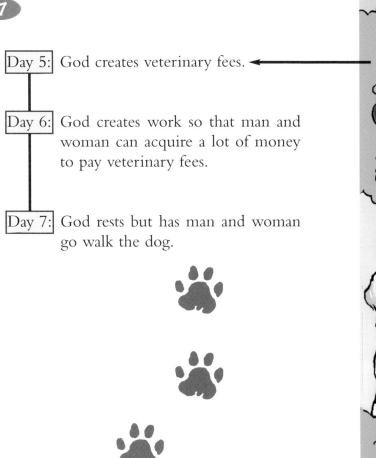

THE BETTER LIVING COUNCIL'S LIST OF TEN THINGS THAT EARLY DOG HAD NO OPPORTUNITY TO BARK AT

1. The whirring, beeping sound of a modem connecting to the Internet

2. Clicks of a tape loading into a VCR

3. Voices coming over the telephone answering machine

4. Recirculating water in hot tubs

5. Rap music

6. Joggers wearing $200 sport shoes

7. Servers in the fast-food, drive-thru window

8. Doorbells

9. Car alarms

10. Pagers and cellular phones

KOKOPELLI'S CREED
ON DOGS AND GARDENS

In regard to a dug-up garden,
an innocent look turns away wrath.

BEAR'S FIRST LAW

A show of affection is the quickest way to get what you want.

THE CANINE THEORY OF DOG DIVERSITY

The best pedigree is one that is mixed.

COMPARATIVE LAW OF CANINE AFFECTION
A cat's love is fleeting;
a dog's is forever.

KOKOPELLI'S DISTINCTION
A dog is adopted,
never purchased.

APPROVED LIST OF CANINE SLEEP HABITATS

1. Head of the bed

2. Foot of the bed

3. Sleeping human's stomach

4. Living room couch

5. Stuffed chair

BEAR'S REVELATION
A lick to the face means more than one to the hand.

THE DRAKE FAMILY'S DISCOVERY
If a low-cost veterinary clinic advertises vaccinations for "under $30.00" be prepared to pay $29.95.

Marking Time—A Poem That Makes "Scents"

—by Bear

From each sturdy fire hydrant
To every stately tree;
From bush to lawn to trash can,
Lift thy leg constantly!

Roll on every new toy;
Press thy snout 'gainst each windowpane;
Spread thy scent throughout the world;
Leave no unmarked terrain!

BEAR'S GOURMET BELIEF
It tastes better after you drag it through the dirt.

SECOND PRINCIPLE OF CANINE DINING
Food from the dog dish
will taste better if eaten
directly off the floor.

THREE UNIVERSAL NEEDS OF DOGS

1. Food

2. Shelter

3. Beef-basted chews

THE ANDERSON FAMILY'S FIRST LAW OF GROOMING SALONS

No matter which day you take a dog to be groomed, the discounted grooming will be offered on another day.

FIRST UNIVERSAL RULE FOR PUPPIES

In all actions, lead with the mouth.

THE KAGEL FAMILY WARNING
There is no such thing as fur that does not shed.

BEAR'S CLARIFICATION
Dogs have personalities; temperaments are for people.

THE CANINE CONGRESS'S PRIMARY TRAINING TIP FOR BUSY HUMANS
To raise a dog to be his best, spend twice as much time with him.

KOKOPELLI'S TOP TEN PSYCHOLOGICAL REASONS WHY DOGS DIG IN THE DIRT

1. OPTIMISM: Feeling that there has to be something really great under all that dirt

2. PESSIMISM: Coming to the conclusion that everything is ugly and ought to be buried anyway

3. AVOIDISM: Trying to escape to a place where humans can't find you

4. CODEPENDENCY: A compulsion to put at least two of you into the same sad hole

5. OBSESSION: A need to get all this digging done once and for all

6. PARANOIA: Realizing that no place is truly safe and that you'd better create a new place "they" won't find

7. MANIC-DEPRESSION: Finding happiness in digging dirt, then realizing it's only moving dirt and quitting; then rationalizing that it's cool to move dirt and going back to do more; then finding it's still the same old dirt and giving up again; then...

8. INSECURITY: The concern that if you're not actively doing something, nobody will love you

9. SCHIZOPHRENIA: Craving to create meaningful holes but at the same time needing to fill them back up again

10. DENIAL: What digging?

THE MATHEMATICS AND MECHANICS OF THE FREE-WALKING DOG
2 zigs + 3 zags = 1 doggy straight line

BEAR'S POSTULATE
The smaller they are, the louder they bark.

THE VOGEL FAMILY'S LAW OF DIMINISHED RESULTS
You can dog proof the inside of your home—almost.

THE CANINE AFFECTION SELECTION RULE
In meeting new people, choose to jump up on the best-dressed one.

BEAR'S "WORDS TO LIVE BY" FOR PUPPIES
Ankles are for biting; wrists are for chewing.

THE CANINE RECREATION COUNCIL'S MORNING INDICATOR FOR INTERACTIVE PLAYTIME

The human act of putting on socks in the morning is a dog's invitation to play tug-of-war.

BEAR'S FOOD CLASSIFICATION SYSTEM

Between the classifications of "leftovers" and "garbage," there should be a step designated as "for the dog."

FROM *UNDERSTANDING HUMANS: YOUR FIELD
GUIDE TO THEIR STRANGE WORLD*
POSITION PAPER G-1: MEETING AND GREETING

The two-legged human is an odd
breed. You may have heard that men
are from Mars and that women
are from Venus. This could
explain a lot. Neither
planet offered the
sensible environment
that our dog planet,
Pluto, did. We were
fortunate to come
from an advanced place.

From the beginning, dogs have developed a highly sophisticated system of identification and greeting. We are naturally blessed with the social nose-pressing and butt-sniffing traits that serve as foolproof salutations. These greetings tell you all you need to know about someone. Unfortunately, due to an inbred defect or a cultural deprivation (possibly caused by that Mars/Venus thing), the two-leggeds seem incapable of making proper introductions. Strive for understanding. Your tolerance and goodwill may go a long way in bringing the two-legged species up to snuff, or sniff as the case may be.

FOURTH LAW OF "THE WALK"
Attempt to meet everybody.

BEAR'S ACRONYM
The initial letters in "Chase All Those" spell *CAT*.

Bernie the Pug's Pugnacious Poem on Pug Appearances

A proper nose–dapper and small,
A jaw set tenacious and bold.
Full, round eyes,
Strong, sturdy teeth:
A perfect face, if truth be told!

Yet I must insist
That the points are all missed
By some humans, misguided thereof,
Who although quite unfair,
Are heard to declare,
"That's a face only a mother could love!"

THE ALTERNATE RULE OF STORAGE

In lieu of a garden,
bury it in a bed.

FIRST TENET OF CANINE LIFE

Find the most awful
thing and sniff it.

KOKOPELLI'S TWO THINGS IN THE UNIVERSE THAT DEFY COMMON SENSE
Black holes and cats

BEAR'S TWO-STEP GUIDE FOR COPING IN THE WORLD

1. Don't let the little things get to you.

2. Don't let the big things get to you.

THE ZELMAN FAMILY'S MORNING MAXIM
The sooner the bed is made, the sooner the dog can get on it.

THE CANINE FREEDOM OF AFFECTION ACT

Neither the size of the dog nor the size of the lap shall be the defining factor in what constitutes a lap dog.

FIRST LAW OF MULTIDOG HOMES

Whatever one dog wants to do (i.e. jump on guests, play fetch, run out a door, etc.), all the dogs want to do at the same time.

BEAR'S MISCHIEF MAXIM

The nicer the clothes, the more fun it is to jump up on the person wearing them.

THE GRAYBER FAMILY'S RULE OF CANINE PHYSICS

There exists a magnetic attraction between a dog's muddy paws and a light-colored, living room couch.

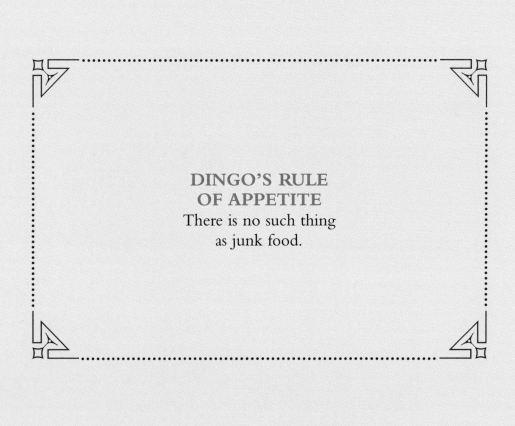

**DINGO'S RULE
OF APPETITE**
There is no such thing
as junk food.

RAY BRADBURY'S OBSERVATION
Dogs think that every day is Christmas

THE ONOMATOPOETIC DESCRIPTION OF PUPPIES AND TRAINS
Chew-Chew-Chew

PRIMARY RULE OF CANINE MASTICATION
Chew toys. Inhale food.

THE CHEWING COROLLARY
Never waste time chewing that which can be swallowed whole.

DINGO'S BEHAVIORAL CLARIFICATION FOR DOG OWNERS
It may look neurotic to you, but it's simply "well-adjusted" to me.

THE SHEATH FAMILY'S DESIGNATION
The eighth wonder of the world is the successful bathing of a dog indoors.

THE CANINE COUNCIL'S TOP THREE RECOMMENDED POSTBATH ACTIVITIES FOR DOGS

 1. Roll in the dirt

 2. Run through sprinklers

 3. Romp through mud

DINGO'S CANINE REVERSAL
If you can't join 'em, lick 'em.

KOKOPELLI'S CANINE SEMINAR SERIES, TOPIC TWO
Should dogs be required to eat dog food invented by people, when people would never eat people food invented by dogs?

TEN-STEP GUIDE TO BATHING A DOG INDOORS

 1. Locate dog

2. Playfully direct dog into tub, sink, or shower

3. Turn on water

4. Chase and retrieve dog

 5. Place dog into tub, sink, or shower

6. After rechasing and reretrieving dog, convince neighbor, friend, or child to hold onto dog in tub, sink, or shower

7. Spray water on dog

8. After chasing and retrieving dog, and drying neighbor, friend, or child, reposition wet dog into tub, sink, or shower and drop bottle of shampoo

9. Wipe down walls, floor, self, neighbor, friend, or child after dog shakes water off coat and smears shampoo everywhere

10. Coax dog into automobile; drive to groomer

THE FOUR-PUP LITTER LAW
There is no such thing as an only pup.

DINGO'S COROLLARY TO THE FOUR-PUP LITTER LAW
You never nurse alone.

THIRD PRINCIPLE OF CANINE DINING
After three different foods have been rejected, settle for the first food offered.

THE DIMENSIONAL DICTATE
Any couch, chair, or cot should be large enough to accommodate one dog.

AN OPEN LETTER TO PEOPLE FROM THE INTERNATIONAL CANINE CONGRESS

For centuries, primary canine theory has held that humans identify with dogs. Why else would so many of you choose to spend time with a dog who looks just like you? Trying to save money on mirrors? We doubt it. Humans and dogs have bonded.

You can see the canine historical influence everywhere. The unusually odd facial expressions of your human supermodels is taken from the overstated haughtiness of the Afghan hound. Dogs such as the boxer and Airedale terrier exude an air of honor and nobility, which is a lot more than your human politicians do when using the same expressions. More and more dogs and people look alike and walk alike! And for the most part we dogs don't mind.

However, over the past one hundred years or so, the pendulum has shifted our way, and dogs have picked up some things from humans, namely, bad habits. Here we are addressing the droolers and gas-passers of the owner breed. To the best of our knowledge, dogs just didn't do those things until they began to associate with humans! No matter. The point is that unless these activities can be controlled—by both human and canine breeds—the world will become an increasingly unpleasant place to live. Let us find some understanding that will limit our similarities to physical appearances so that both breeds can evolve more elegantly.

DINGO'S SCIENTIFIC DOG AND CAT COMPARISON QUIZ
This comprehensive, humanitarian quiz will once and for all settle a question that has raged throughout humankind since the beginning of time, namely, who's better, cats or dogs?

SECTION A: MULTIPLE CHOICE
Answer each question by circling **C** (for Cat) or **D** (for Dog)

1. Which species is known as "your best friend"?   **C** or **D**

2. Which species is known as "that #!*##!*%! cat"?   **C** or **D**

3. Which species communicates by using a rich, elegant, and operatic *woof*, rather than a shrill, annoying, caterwauling whine?   **C** or **D**

 **4.** Which species is better at:

    a. Catching a Frisbee?   C or D

    b. Playing fetch?   C or D

    c. Sniffing a crotch?   C or D

5. Which species holds the most wins in Iditarod dog sled racing?   C or D

SECTION B: HUMANITARIAN ESSAY
Describe the last time you encountered a Seeing Eye cat.

_____

_____

_____

_____

SCORING: Is there really any question?

**DINGO'S
STATEMENT
ON BREEDS**
The noisiest breed of dog
is the neighbor's.

**DINGO'S
CONTRARIAN THEORY**
If it smells really bad,
it must be really good.

----**FIRST INSTRUCTION FOR LIVING IN A HUMAN WORLD**
You have only one tail; keep it away from children.

2

SECOND INSTRUCTION FOR LIVING IN A HUMAN WORLD
The sound of one bark calls for another.

3 ----**THIRD INSTRUCTION FOR LIVING IN A HUMAN WORLD**
If it can fit in your mouth, bury it.

Take The Dog

DINGO'S THREE-WORD CURE
FOR SEPARATION ANXIETY

DINGO'S ALTERNATE
THREE-WORD CURE FOR
SEPARATION ANXIETY

Just
Don't
Go

THE TAIL-WAGGER'S ILLOGICAL LOGIC

Problem: Statistics show that only one out of three bones buried is ever found again.

Solution: Bury more bones.

THE CANINE ACTIVITY COMMITTEE'S REPORT ON FURNISHINGS

There are only two sizes of doggy doors—too big and too small.

DINGO'S LAMENT
It always takes longer to
beg for it than to eat it.

**DINGO'S REFLECTION ON
THE HUMAN CONDITION**
Only a human would take time
to invent a pooper-scooper.

The Puppy Coalition's Blueprint for a Perfect Puppy

A running, jumping, rolling, "klunk"-ing
Mass of mouth and fur.
Nipping, pawing, chewing, and gnawing,
With your hands the main allure!

DINGO'S REFLECTION

Puppies and babies grow up too fast.

DINGO'S PARADOX
Bark at everything,
even nothing.

**THE CANINE
COUNCIL'S FOURTH
PROPOSAL FOR LIVING**
In the absence of cars to chase,
squirrels and birds make
acceptable substitutes.

FROM *UNDERSTANDING HUMANS: YOUR FIELD GUIDE TO THEIR STRANGE WORLD* POSITION PAPER B-22: THE BALL

Humans seem to always have some sort of ball with them. Research shows that a ball plays a very important role in human existence, even giving birth to such mega-business human enterprises as baseball, basketball, football, and dozens of variations that can employ such balls as bowling balls, soccer balls, tennis balls, and even golf balls, to name a few.

Thus, the human culture cherishes its ball and attaches profound importance to it. As best friends, it befits dogs to respect this odd attachment and guard these possibly religious objects. Yet, here is where the contradictions set in.

Possibly to test our loyalty, or possibly as a result of a momentary derangement, these same humans exhibit a tendency to discard themselves of their ball when in company of a canine! The sacred objects are tossed, thrown forcibly, and hurled into the air and propelled great distances for no apparent reason! Canines for centuries have gone off to retrieve the precious objects and return them to their rightful human.

Reports from canine research psychologists working in the field have shown that when a dog tests a human by electing not to retrieve the ball, the human invariably retrieves it himself, apparently coming to his senses.

Whatever material or spiritual value the human ascribes to the ball, let it be so. The bottom line is that humans seem so happy when we retrieve the silly things for them, and who are we to deny them that?

Dingo's Song of Love

The electric whir of a can opener!
The solid thump of a refrigerator door!
The sacred syllables: Din-ner-time!
Who could ask for anything more?!

DINGO'S RULE OF WILL
A determined dog with a ball in his mouth can still bark.

DINGO'S BATHING BELIEF
The purpose of a bath is to get a human wet and soapy.

ROCKY 'S
PERSONAL VIEW

When the going gets tough,
the tough get going and the poodles cut out.

WILL ROGERS'S DOG'S COMMENT
I never met a table scrap I didn't like

**ROCKY'S FAVORITE
DOWN-HOME PROVERB**
Love me, love my dog.

**ROCKY'S LEAST FAVORITE
DOWN-HOME CLICHÉ**
You're barking up the wrong tree.

THE SEMANTICALLY CORRECT CARDINAL RULE FOR CANINES

Never let your master know you're smarter than he or she is.

ROCKY'S DOWN-HOME WISDOM

Life is a simple dance. You don't need to tango through it when a little two-step will do.

An ounce of prevention comes in the form of shots.

A man's home is his castle, but a woman holds all the keys.

Take time to smell the roses...and the trees...and the bushes...and the fire hydrants...and the grass...and...

**ROCKY'S FIRST
DOWN-HOME
LAW OF BREEDS**
In talking to dachshunds you get
the long and the short of it.

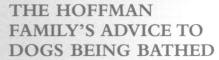

**THE HOFFMAN
FAMILY'S ADVICE TO
DOGS BEING BATHED**
Soap is for washing, not eating.

FIRST RULE OF CAR RIDES
Find the driver's lap and sit there.

SECOND RULE OF CAR RIDES
Claim the open window and face the wind.

THIRD RULE OF CAR RIDES
When all other areas become boring, lie above the backseat,
against the rear window.

ROCKY'S ROADHOUSE RECIPE FOR HAPPINESS

Be glad you are whatever you are (even if you're a cat).

Accept others as whatever they are.

Remember that it can always get worse (or better).

Believe in yourself. What have you got to lose?

Enthusiasm will get you farther than a pedigree will.

Call on the big dog within.

Understated is worth more than overblown.

Explain nothing. Let them figure you out.

THE FENDER FAMILY'S EXCEPTION TO THE RULES OF BUDGETING

If it's for the dog, out comes the checkbook.

BEAR'S BACKUP

Never send a poodle to do a
Labrador retriever's job.

FIRST LAW OF PHOTOGRAPHING DOGS

The dog's best pose comes immediately
after you've run out of film.

One to two full-body, all-out, head-first, bolting charges

Four strict two-step stop-and-sniffs

Two to three 360-degree leash turns around ankles

For maximum body building benefits, load carbohydrates (dry food) before the workout and replace proteins (wet food) after the workout.

THE CALLARD FAMILY'S FOURTH RULE OF THE HOUSEHOLD
If it's unbreakable, the dog won't knock it over.

KOKOPELLI'S PROFOUND QUESTION
Should a cat's age be measured in dog years?

ROCKY'S RULE OF CLEANLINESS
If there is a single puddle in the backyard, your dog will find it.

THIRD LAW OF MOBILITY
Whenever possible, lie down.

**CHERYL'S
ANTIGRAMMATICAL
RULE OF DOGS
AND DATING**
If the dog don't like 'em,
don't date 'em.

FIRST COMFORTING PRINCIPLE FOR THE WANDERING DOG

If you know that you're at a place, even if it's not this place or that place, you're someplace, and that means you're not really lost.

**ROCKY'S
RULE
OF THE WALK**
The most interesting trees are always
in somebody else's yard.

**ROCKY'S
UNDERSTANDING OF
THE HUMAN WORLD**
An open gate is an invitation
to run through it.

EIGHT GREAT REASONS WHY INTELLIGENT PEOPLE PREFER THE COMPANY OF DOGS TO OTHER PEOPLE

 1. Dogs don't care about your makeup, your clothes, or whether you've gained 10 pounds

2. Dogs are not obsessed with healing their wounded inner puppy.

3. Dogs don't try to impress you with fast cars or money.

4. Dogs don't hog the remote.

5. When you call a dog, you're never put on hold or offered a menu of other options.

6. Dogs don't make you fill out forms in triplicate.

7. The only place a dog will tell you to go is on a walk.

8. Dogs never become lawyers.

Kokopelli's Salute to the Canine Work Ethic

Herding, guarding, Seeing Eye,
Sports, or search and rescue.
Dogs hold jobs of every kind.
What does a stupid cat do?

WORK?!

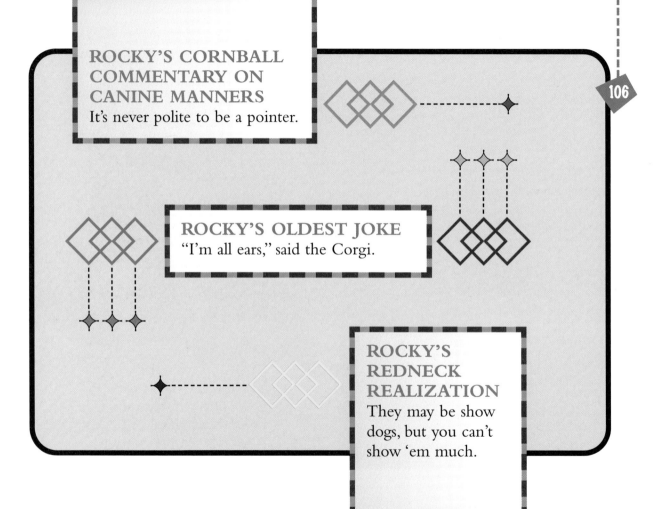

ROCKY'S CORNBALL COMMENTARY ON CANINE MANNERS
It's never polite to be a pointer.

ROCKY'S OLDEST JOKE
"I'm all ears," said the Corgi.

ROCKY'S REDNECK REALIZATION
They may be show dogs, but you can't show 'em much.

**FIRST PRINCIPLE
OF CANINE KISSES**
The bigger and sloppier
the kiss, the better it is.

THE CANINE KISS COMPARISON
A kiss from a dog will never give you a cold.

THE RANCH HOUSE AXIOM
If you can reach it, you can chew it.

ARTICLE 33 FROM THE CANINE LINGUISTIC INFORMATION FORUM
The words *come here* mean that the human uttering them will soon be walking toward you.

THE CANINE COMMISSION'S FIRST STATISTICAL ANALYSIS
Ninety percent of owners believe they are in charge.
The other ten percent know the truth.

THE DUTY ROSTER
OFFICIAL JOBS AND DUTIES TO BE PERFORMED
DAILY IN THE HUMAN WORLD
ISSUED BY CANINE CENTRAL COMMAND

1. General Daylight Duty: Bark at anything you see, even if it's nothing.

5. Sleeping, napping, and resting are prime duties and supersede all of the above.

2. General Nightshift Duty: Bark at anything you hear, even if it's yourself.

4. During travel: Thrust your head out of any open window and watch diligently for oncoming traffic.

3. Twice daily: Sit at attention and beg for food. Once daily: Execute a generic whimper routine in order to see what you can get.

ROCKY'S SECRET ADVICE TO DOGS
Never let your humans know you understand
everything they're saying.

BEAR'S ADDITION
...or thinking!

FOON'S COROLLARY
Never pounce on
a cat with white
stripes down
her back.

ROCKY'S FIRST LESSON OF NATURE
Skunks are meant to be
chased, not caught.

ROCKY'S NEW LAWS OF THE CANYON
(AFTER THE DOGS TAKE OVER)

❋ Those god-awful cackling rooster calls shall be replaced with elegant, deep-throated, wake-up woofs.

❋ The distinctions between dog food and people food shall be abolished and be replaced by one equal form of "down-home cookin'."

❋ All cats shall be confined to stables and barns to do honest labor—hunting field mice.

❋ The right-of-way on horse trails shall be granted to dogs.

❋ Trespassing dogcatchers shall be arrested and presumed guilty. Then lynched.

TRIGGER'S FIRST RULE
OF TRAVEL FOR HUMANS
If you can't take your pets,
it's not worth going.

**THIRD CANINE
RULE OF THE
OUTDOORS**
Keep sniffing. You never
know what you'll find.

**TRIGGER'S
CANINE LAW
FOR HUMANS**
When in doubt,
scratch the back.

**TRIGGER'S DELINEATION
BETWEEN CATS AND DOGS**
Cats know how to say *please*, but only
dogs know how to say *thank you*.

Why can't cats just learn to say *good~bye*?"

**FIRST CANON
OF CANINE
RESPONSIBILITY**
All the world is a
territory, and all
territory must
be marked.

TRIGGER'S ADVICE TO PUPPIES
To keep on the good side of a master, never chew shoes that still have feet in them.

FIRST PRINCIPLE OF POLITICALLY CORRECT CANINE TERMINOLOGY
Never use the word *mutt* when *mixed breed* is meant.

TRIGGER'S TRUISM
The best time during the day to eat is all day.

KOKOPELLI'S ADDITION
The sound of a can opener brings music to the ears.

TRIGGER'S THREE-STEP TERRITORIAL GUIDE

1. View the area

2. Sniff the area

3. Mark the area

THE UNIVERSAL CANINE COMMISSION'S
HIERARCHY OF TRICKS
DOG GUIDELINES TO PERFORMANCE AND FEES

Since the first *Homo sapiens* threw the first dinosaur bones for their canine companions to "fetch" (then switched to throwing rocks after dogs buried the bones), humankind has been relentless in its search for new mindless activities to engage in with dogs.

It thus became necessary to categorize activities dogs were expected to engage in and set up a corresponding fee schedule.

The Labor Council of the Universal Canine Commission drafted these guidelines for ensuring equality in the workplace.

THIRD-DEGREE TRICKS

Trick or Task
- Sleeping on the bed
- Lying on living room floor
- Avoidance of passing gas
  following big meals

Compensation
- Continued quiet
- Not being tripped over
- 1 Pat on the Head
  plus 1 low-fat dog biscuit

SECOND-DEGREE TRICKS

Trick or Task
- Lying down after being told to sit
- Sitting after being told to come
- Staring into space after being told "fetch!"

Compensation
- 1 treat
- 1 treat, plus praise
- ½ treat

FIRST-DEGREE TRICKS

Trick or Task
- Walking on-leash, in circles,
  around human legs
- Barking at the front door
- Watching a thrown Frisbee
  fall to the ground

Compensation
- 1½ pieces of sandwich meat
- 2 treats
- 1 treat, plus praise

THIRD CARDINAL RULE FOR CANINES
That which is sniffed once, must be sniffed again.

RULE OF KNOWLEDGE
You can teach an old dog new tricks, but only if he feels like learning them.

THE LAWSON FAMILY'S RULE OF PURCHASE
After paying full-price for a premium brand of dog food, you will find a discount coupon for the item.

TRIGGER'S CREED
Fences are made for jumping; doors are made to run through.

THE BAKER FAMILY RULE OF THE HOUSE

If it's on the floor and small enough to roll under a chair, it will eventually end up in the dog's mouth.

RULE OF TIMING

The day after you get your trim is the day the weather turns cold.

THE MITCHELL FAMILY'S THEORY

The more elaborate the doghouse, the less it will be used.

PRIMARY RULE OF CANINE/HUMAN COMMUNICATION

Any sentence not containing the word *dinner* can be ignored.

CANINE CULTURAL COMPARISON CHART

1950s Dog
- Attracted to fire hydrants ——————————
- Chews on twigs and rope ——————————
- Buries bones ——————————
- Fed leftover beef jerky ——————————

- Responds to master's voice ——————————
- Terrorizes mailman ——————————
- Is your very best friend ——————————

New Millennium Dog
- Attracted to bottled-water stands
- Chews on computer cables and modem connections
- Buries the remote
- Fed biodegradable, sodium-free, low-fat, aspic-flavored, beef-basted rawhide
- Responds to master's pager
- Terrorizes mail carrier
- Is your very best friend

Trigger's Tribute to Kibbles

A mountain of kibbles awaits in my dish;
There must be thirty or more!
But nothing beats moving them one-by-one
And eating them off the floor!

TRIGGER'S DISTINCTION
There are two kinds of dog toys: those that must be guarded and those that must be ignored.

THE CORY FAMILY'S OBSERVATION
The smaller the kitchen, the more likely the dog will choose the middle of it for a nap.

SECOND RULE OF BEDTIME ETIQUETTE
Take only half of your human's bed—the middle half.

SECOND RULE FOR GETTING WHAT YOU WANT
Let your eyes and a whimper do the talking.

TRIGGER'S COMMON SENSE RULE
After you break it, stop chewing on it.

THE SECOND COMMANDMENT FOR PUPPIES
Chase thy tail.

TRIGGER'S SCOOP ON PUPPIES
In housebreaking and business you've got to complete all the paperwork.

THE CANINE NUTRITION LEAGUE'S
CHEWING CHART FOR PUPPIES

This chart is provided as an instructional guide to the prime cuts of your human's "running shoe" (a.k.a. chew toy). While aged shoes provide more dirt and protein, a fresh shoe makes for a more eye-pleasing presence. Garnish with grass for a completely balanced chew.

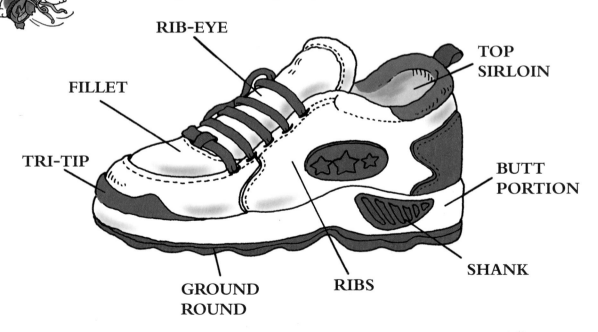

RIB-EYE

TOP SIRLOIN

FILLET

TRI-TIP

BUTT PORTION

SHANK

GROUND ROUND

RIBS

THE CANINE RECREATION COMMISSION'S GUIDE TO BEACHES

Beaches and shorelines are unique and confusing environments for dogs. The following time-tested principles should serve as guides in governing your canine beach behavior.

 FIRST PRINCIPLE
Meet all incoming waves head-on and bite them.

 SECOND PRINCIPLE
Run! Run! Then run some more!

 THIRD PRINCIPLE
Those large white, gray, or brown things with wings and funny feet are seagulls. They are there for you to chase.

FOURTH PRINCIPLE
Ignore balls, toys, and Frisbees thrown into the surf. Retrieve only kelp and seaweed.

 FINAL PRINCIPLE
At the end of day, transport as much sand as physically possible to the backseat of the owner's vehicle and distribute it thoroughly.

Bob Lovka is a Southern California-based writer whose work includes poetry, satire, humor books and calendars, and television, script, and stage show writing. Bob's connection to felines and canines keeps expanding. Homeless cats and dogs look him up constantly, and uncannily they have increased their appearances since Bob wrote *The Splendid Little Book of All Things Cat* and *The Splendid Little Book of All Things Dog*. Many of these animals have found homes through Bob's association with Angel Puss and Pooch Rescue. Bob is owned by a cat and is tormented by a jealous Lhasa apso who "authored" this book.

Photo by Joy Edwards

Photo by Rick Broderick

Setsu Broderick's illustrations, decorative designs, and commercial artwork are seen throughout the world. Her whimsical and charming original creations have been turned into collectibles, music boxes, plush toys, books, and figurines. She has illustrated two books, *The Splendid Little Book of All Things Cat* and *The Splendid Little Book of All Things Dog*. Max, her desk-chewing cockatoo, remains her most vocal art critic.